NIGHTSHIFT WORKERS

NIGHTSHIFT
WORKERS

GEORGE CHARLTON

BLOODAXE BOOKS

ISBN: 1 85224 070 9

First published 1989 by
Bloodaxe Books Ltd,
P.O. Box ISN,
Newcastle upon Tyne NE99 ISN

Bloodaxe Books Ltd acknowledges
the financial assistance of Northern Arts.

Typesetting by Bryan Williamson, Manchester.

Printed in Great Britain by
Bell & Bain Limited, Glasgow, Scotland.

To Susan, Alex and James

Acknowledgements

Acknowledgements are due to the editors of the following publications in which some of these poems first appeared: *Bad Seed, Bananas, Blue Lion, Caret, the Echo Room, Evening Chronicle* (Newcastle), *Harry's Hand, Here Now, London Magazine, Meridian, New Angles 2* (Oxford University Press, 1987), *New Poetry 2* (Arts Council, 1976), *Stand* and *Very Green.*

Some of these poems first appeared in a pamphlet, *The Lost Boys* (Echo Room Press, 1986), and some in Neil Astley's anthology *Ten North-East Poets* (Bloodaxe Books, 1980). Several have also been broadcast by Tyne-Tees Television.

'Dividends' was joint first prize winner in the Newcastle *Evening Chronicle* Poetry Competition in 1984.

The cover shows a detail from *The Pit Road* by Norman Cornish, reproduced by kind permission of the artist and Tyne and Wear Museums Service

Contents

A Return to Newcastle

I'm up from the South and back to it:
Brown Ale in the cryptic pubs full
Of the lilt of Geordie accents.
A frog-prince back, too thirsty for release
From terraced streets' truncated ends,
Those old bricked-off perspectives.

Under roof tops hatched like herringbone
Jobless men read paperbacks till dawn
At a loss. Time-served engineers
Done with the sea, return to river towns –
Prodigal salmon spawning in the Tyne,
That unrepeatable, one-off gesture.

As a youth on a summer Saturday night
I waited in a shop door for a girl,
Head into the sports page. In those days
A soft curve could draw the eye downwards
Where Grey Street, tawny in late sun,
Defined its limits – my own inelegance.

Nightshift Workers

They have come from a factory
Where fluorescent strips flared all night

And ears grew numb to machinery.
They are going home to working wives,

To cooling beds at breakfast time,
Undressing fatigue from their skin like clothes.

Later to wake at four and taste teeth
Soft as fur in their mouths.

They live in a dislocation of hours
Inside-out like socks pulled on in darkness

Waking when the day is over.
They are always at an ebb, unlike others

Going out to work in the morning
Where sun and moon shine in the sky together.

Sea Coal

This is the coal coast. Where Seaham tilts seawards
Splintered suns float on the North Sea's pressure
Compounding best coal squeezed from strata

Between seafloor and rockbed. Below,
Sunken eyes lie back exhausted;
Cold currents unpick the sinews of men

Who rippled in earnest, coaling Imperial flotillas:
Both bone-cage and bulkhead fronds
Have fossilised in sea-salt.

Underwater siftings are washing
From the stokehold of the sea, poor nuts,
For sea coal burns badly, gives off meagre heat.

It has become derelict treasure salvaged
Out of an undertow. Coal has produced
Its own decay: coal-pickers who scrounge

Bent-backed on the water-fringe, balance
Sacks on the cross-bars of clapped-out bikes,
Stretch their spines and look out gazing –

There dead things have come from the sea to tell
Bleached tales to the hard-up and out of work,
Rumouring of desolation riding the slack.

Man on a Roof

He is up on a roof with the sun,
A cauldron of bitumen frothing
In the street far below. I see him

From my window, diminished
As a climber on an ice-face.
His tools are a trowel and a minute pick.

Raising slates like the lid of a box
He peeps in on lofts
Dusty as coal-workings caught in sunlight

Or, with mild fists, casts about,
Aching for whispering laths, for the squeak
And the crack of each flawed slate –

The man-avalanche that would be himself.

Rooney's Rainbow

And there it was —
A rainbow in Rooney's scrapyard
Effervescent in the morning sun,
A pick-me-up among
Cast-iron, worn out machinery:
A red carpet of rust petals,
Wilted propellers — the liquidated
Dreams of industrial dynasties.

It's a crock of hard cash for Rooney
In his made-to-measure dark blue suit
And freckled brogues, a fat Havana
Cigar clutched in his paw.

Dividends

Redundant, the coal-staithes
Look down on themselves
Into a tainted river.
On the banks above, earthmovers
Have dispersed the human smells
That once belonged to rooms –
A waste ground of wild purple flowers
No one now claims to own.

But in the modern flats
A kilowatt bar outshines
The evening sun...
A mother's gossip with a daughter
Continues after dark.

And her man walks with a stick
As if he could be back
Forty years and swaggering
When love, or something like it,
Oozed through the cracks in the paving.

Friday Evening

The evening star sparks
Struck like a welding arc.

In dull light of the varnished pubs
Young men wait, scrubbed clean as water-babies,

The thought of work almost dismissed
And leisure compromised.

Here and there a moustache soft as lichen
Moistens on the white head of a beer,

Cigarettes congest the ashtrays
Silted as their smoke-fouled mouths.

Mass participants in drink
These heroes of the commonplace

Anticipate the casual girls –
The ever-expanding universe

Hurrying to a party,
Its platonic, its adulterated love.

Another Friday Evening

In the snug plush of executive suites
Photocopiers flicker, clinically green,
As strict accountants, late at work,
Apply those final touches to the books –
The feint lines on their pinstripe suits
Repeated on the pages in a leather-bound ledger.

While mopping up tight corners,
At the right angles of corridors, carbolicky
Cleaners take a long-shanked partner
And quick-slow the foxtrot, faultily,
As the jug-jug of a discotheque rises
Dull in the colon of a deep wine bar.

For already and down town so soon,
Shirt-sleeved in October weather
Come the slim, ectomorphic lads,
Dodging as they go their way
The droppings made by starlings
On pavements and on low walls –
A smell fermenting after rain,
A fine fluff infecting the lungs.

Durham Miners' Gala

Grandfather told me that Gala Day
How during the days of the General Strike
The miners' band played for the tranquil soldiers
From regiments at bivouac in the meadows;
How out beyond the ends of double-rows
Expectant policemen simmered
Frustrated in their function.

                       Buzzed by flies
Grandfather drank dark beer, sprawled
On grass green as the blinked sun.

That Gala Day the blue patrols picked up the rowdy drunks –
Miners, their skin translucent blue as ghosts
Who'd marched behind the colliery bands.
Lodge banners, so silky that they gleamed like coal,
Lay curled up in their mottoes of
Wesley's vision of Methodist peace.

It was grandfather's last time out.
And there I was, helping an old man home.

Hunting the Hare

The electric hare is orbiting a track
Floodlit as the bright side of the moon.
Hounds uncoil from traps, intuitive
Experts in pursuit and slaughter...
And these working men this night
Are the aristocrats of Odds.

Their cluttered living rooms,
The belly-aching, boss-eyed wives who watch
Dull coal collapse into the ticking grates
Are not a part of this. This
Is the Eldorado of men's dreams.
They could return tonight,
Chancellors bearing free gifts for the family.

In a shining sky the full moon's face
Has an imprint of the hare on it.

The Pigeon Fancier

Folk tattle by to Windy Nook,
A dawdling of washing in the lane

Where he stands at the cree's open door,
His coat and his bait-bag slung

From the nail in a post.
Poised tiptoe on verandah planks

He rattles morse in a tin of pellets:
Coded commands only pigeons can crack...

The whole scope of him is on the sky
As those plump blips vector home

For the brief display of pigeon heroics –
A jumbo-nimble bank, a glide,

And – for a finish, at his bidding –
The plummet to the ducket.

Retired Men

They live in a silent factory,
In an atmosphere of truce –
Houses muted, windows glazed with dust.

Today at this spectacle –
The show of the sea – they are alone,
Or with families on economy returns.

Exhausted like second-hand settees
Sea-noise stuns them,
Continuous machinery.

Unambitious people, they are
Finished with the excellence of skills.
Killing time, they have time to kill.

Pat Buckly's Bequest

There was a widow – and a Morris van
To be auctioned at the bargain sale.

And tools on racks in the lock-up garage –
Still there, quietly rusting.

There were potato plants in the allotment
Gone to seed where the rank weeds prosper.

And there were tales of the fighting at Arnhem,
And his final appointments

At hospital: it was there
They found work in him yet.

Gipsies

They haven't found a permanent site
For the gipsies: they park on waste ground.

The wiry men have eyes that stare
Beyond any alcoholic daze –

Their kids are scruffy and abuse us,
Or else ask for money.

They are no longer like picturesque photographs
Of robust men grinning on clay pipes,

No longer living in caravans
That appeal to our imagination.

That unconstrained happiness
Of a century ago

Has resolved itself into these arguments
With a wife whose belly bulges out her frock.

They appear to do nothing all day.
They are not like us. We do not want to be them.

Some weeks later the Council tipped
Rubbish on their site: they moved on.

Postcard Poems

The Kiss

Tucking his nose away across her cheek
Her nose against his cheek
Lips pressing lips – tongue sucking tongue,
His tongue along the smooth edge of her teeth
Her mouth warm as an oven, cool as peach:

An inconsolable happiness!

Morning Sickness

A mother-to-be pukes into the pan.
Out of sympathy I do the same,
Woken from a kind of sleep that leaves you exhausted.
It is that time of morning things are most acute.
It's as if we'd lost our sense of humour.

AWOL

It is that we never lived together
In those rented rooms at the city's edge –
The bed a love-pit, books a barricade.
It is that we never married,
Secretly in the rain,
A few friends for witnesses,
The calendar changed from that date.

No. I was a deserter on the by-roads all along.

Telephones

Their lips are cold,
They do not breathe in your ear.
With digital hearts
Worn on their sleeves
They cannot be persuaded of anything.

Single-minded as cats
They leave you in the end,
Returned purring to their cradles.

Jugged Hare

It is an odd number,
An incomplete equation
Your absence – that warm indifference
Absorbent like the softest tissue paper.

Vivid it blooms, tropical vegetation
Sustained throughout a wet season.
Needles of rain are probing
A self-inflicted wound.

Contact is useless sentiment,
Mildewed hope.
On a short walk to the corner shop
I piece it back together, bit by bit.

Wilt

The interminable term and you
Passing before me daily,
Hip-level…My eyes rise
No higher than your collarbone,
Besieged in the desk-love of teachers:
And you – free and going home.

Mixing Drinks

He waits in a car, window wound down,
Elbow at rest, and his chin in a palm.

Or he sits at table, nonplussed for the girl,
Sipping the brim of the glass in his hand –

A chilled, dry white wine,
A cascade of soda scaling the walls.

At the place words fail there are instead
Booze and tobacco on his frozen tongue.

But the wine: the wine he is bibbing slowly...
Festina lente, that's the style!

The Faerie Queene

It is a wonderful feeling, internal bleeding.
When an apprehensive cold might tingle
The surface of the hard things in a room
There is warmth in the pit of the stomach
Spreading, under blankets – the lungs
Working fitfully, and dreams manoeuvering
Below the tension of the eyelids...
And all because of you, Liz, Bess,
Whatever your name is now –
Eyelids powdered lightly, just a trace
Of the stick, like blood, on your lips.

Tadger's Spark

That night Tadger hurt his eye
We stood at the bonfire –
Someone already had called for an ambulance,
And his moans came quietly
As if he were trying
To work things out for himself.

For comfort an old wife had come
Out of the cold and the dark,
And on to the ground lit
In the ring of the fire.
She told the tale of a riveter –
How that man who could swing

A tenpound, long-shanked hammer,
Went home odd evenings from the yard,
A dirty fist screwed into the socket
Of an eye, and wept keen tears
All night – a steel splinter lodged
Between the jelly and the lid.

She stood in a printed pinafore dress,
Arms folded across her breasts,
Shifting her wasted bulk
From one bare leg to another;
And turned to face the fire's glare,
Tadger's spark split in her eye.

Tadger's Apprenticeship

Your tools have been stowed tonight
   beside the salty metals,
amongst their rusting tangs.
   You have scrubbed clean those hands
the crabbing cold skinned,
   craft-hands, not needed tonight
as you chugged from pub to bar.
   You have been forgetful of snow
as it fell on the Tyne,
   the gantry's silence where you sang,
nor have you seen –
   unzipped at the back of an engine shed –
a snow-grey destroyer
   in for a refit and sneaking
to its berth: nor, necessarily,
   have you heard the *whute*
whute of its siren –
   green birds shook out
from the slick regimes of leaf
   but closer, as you might imagine.

Gateshead Grammar

There must be hundreds like us now,
Born since the war, brought up
In terraced streets near factory yards
And on expansive council estates.

We were the ones who stayed on at school
In academic quarantine. Others
Took apprenticeships in the skilled trades
And left us indoors to finish homework.

And we didn't notice it at first –
All the literature that wasn't written
For us: passing an exam
Was an exercise in its own right.

To live like Spartans, think like monks
Had something heroic about it...
Now we dress carefully, and at
Introductions in expensive restaurants

Suppress the local accent in our voice,
Not to give ourselves away.
And little by little we go home less
To parents who seem to have fostered us:

We are like those bankrupt millionaires
With our own social success stories
And personal failures. Remaindered
Fashions at give-away prices.

Question and Answer

For an instant and
Abolishing himself,
A chameleon in the classroom.

A vision of such light
Merely by being there:
His adenoidal eyes,
His mute catechism –

And his tongue, Joe,
Coiled round the big words
As if mouthing
A difficult language.

The Avenues

It was, as usual, déjà-vu:
Those streets repeating
Themselves, the park's leafy mystery
At the end of each street,
And our football rebounding
Seven leagues from the wall.
As always, the usual kiddie,
A drunk in minature, swigging Coke
Would ask who we were
Or blow the perfect spit-ball,
While on a windowsill a brindled cat
Remained entranced in its furry bowl,
And a lank girl signalled
The usual, skirt held aside
As the bleak boyfriend stood by.
And I would chance an arm
If only to stop the ball –
That own-goal you'd scored already
Against the *For Sale* board at your
Front door.

Singleton

I imagine your father married
The girl late in life, and that
For your matron-mother at the children's home

You were a child she longed for.
You shared in the shift of shared toys
So becoming mild and sure –

Ate meals at long tables
With enough friends for a ship's company.
Even then it seemed voyages

With imaginary companions
You created to confide in,
Who when the small-talk ended were gone.

Though you still have that separateness
Only-children recognise –
An alone, not lonely presence,

In the early morning you find
A strange friend at the wash-basin
Who is not a brother you know.

In a Sunlit Bar

Three days of sun and the girls
Have a lobster finish – necks flushed pink.

Evasive, nubile bodies,
They trot to the toilet in pairs –

In tandem like little seahorses...
And the famished eyes of a barman

Follow as they go.
Gaudy puritan in a neat shell-jacket,   .

His smile is a permanent fiction
Where municipal pigeons flirt on a window-ledge,

And a couple sitting in a corner
Are reconciled to sunlight –

Manic mongrels of indeterminate status
They are nose to nose, wagging tails.

In the Lit & Phil

The Spirit of Inquiry lives on
Here, beside the inventor Swan's
Electric incandescent lamp
And Boer War histories, mildew-damp.
A fad, a quirk, a hobby-horse –
A long-served schoolmaster's curse
At some intemperate article
In a weekly periodical...
Here fragile students dream they fail
Examinations once again,
Teasing tobacco from a tin
At the placid oval table,
Where stoical chairs seem to suffer
The hurt of something hard to bear.
And adolescent, broaching forty,
This would be where I come in...ah!
In shock, as leaving a cinema
In too broad, too brilliant daylight,
Wrestling with a baby carriage,
Beneath the smile of Mr Parish
Greeting again the bairns and wife.

Correspondence

I was there at the bridge
Watching gulls crashland
On the river, all those miles inland,
Wondering what it was
That brought them up so far –
When I saw you stepping down
The other bank, familiar
In your greens and browns.

I had come back, evacuee
From a disaster area,
Imagining this time –
Closer than the letters
We exchanged, further
Than the freckles on your hand.

The Bathing Class

The boy has propped his head upon his arm
Apparently absorbed in the bathers.
He's given us the cold shoulder, dreaming
Of private incomes that made them lazy.

In an art that's left nothing to chance,
Those younger sons of petty bourgeoisie
Inherit life from a month of Sundays –
A world subdued to its granular calm.

The Lost Boys

They are here in quayside bars
By moonlight, their South American mustachios
Reminiscent of the places they'd take off to
If they could, career prospects blown.

Outside, a wall-eyed moon hangs round
In a night of green fog, and the ghostly ships
Await their embarkation
For the pale relief of the guano islands.

The water, not far off, keeps up
A muffled agitation with itself
Like advice given by acquaintances
Who could not grow up or settle down.

They have loved a lot of people
In their time, too many perhaps
To have done themselves good,
And appear not to have changed in years

As they sit at tables like the gods
In postures of exhaustion. Fatigue
Has smudged their eyes, their public bar democracy
And franchise lasts till closing time.

Singing in the Bath

Sunlight this winter afternoon
Frosted through a breath of steam

Picks out unfinished paintwork,
Shelves cleared of your deodorants.

I'm lathered in the foam of soap you left,
Knotty leg-nerves soothed,

The working parts at ease...
I'm singing in the bath

Till the blooms of scum accumulate –
Singing deep, and flat – singing along

With the hot-tank's dyspeptic
Watery accompaniment.

Cloud Bursts

In the tops of tall trees
Rooks are at
Their domestic quarrels again...
And you, in out of the rain,
Warm and wet,
The kagoule glistening,
Your bare legs like sliced white pears.

Don't worry. In a short while
It will be over.
The window-pane is mended,
The geranium's in its pot.
A missel thrush stares out
From beneath a bush.

Ouseburn Emblems

The spider, a mixed bag of nerves,
Is leaving her woof, is leaving her loom.
She is taking early retirement –
Skedaddling the ever-thrumming web
On twitchy, cross-country legs.

*

At last, exasperated wasps
Abort an aerial reconnaissance
Above the lounge-bar counter –
Surviving such a flak barrage
Of silently exploding blooms
They touch down to refuel.

*

Dragonflies plying at evening
The clumped viridian islands...
Amongst those shades, a pulse of dewlap,
The voices of dun toads. They are –
Stolid burghers of the walled
And moated flowerbed,
The interred concrete citadel –
Supercilious at moon-rise.

*

And the burn is psalmed to sleep
By the tussle
Of its own restlessness
On the bed it has made for itself,
Beneath that moon which is ghost
To the hare – quizzical
Executor of a late bequest:
    Lost fields, ancient
    Boundaries by the acre.

This Evening

Arc lamps along the motorway this evening
Bristle in an evening world,
Close to the estate – yet they might as well be
A nebulous n-thousand miles
From a bedroom and its privacies.

There, nightly and night-long, couples perhaps
Can occupy the thick of it – an infectious crisis
Absent from the catalogues,
Their faces lit like the sun-flushed moon
Above a bungalow and a maisonette
As yet too new to be ghost-inhabited.

And should they abhor silence,
Then the telephone might chirrup like a cricket,
A notion of wind tug at the door
As though someone had come home,
Pulling slowly from the slip road,
And brought with them, to a place such as this,
Sweetness – smooth, and powdery as plaster, and raw.

A Couple I Might Know

I would think I understand their ways:
The way, for example, her clear wide gaze

Can take him in. And the way his love
Might be a straight forward reflex action –

The kick-start of a motorcycle
On which he has taken her up,

Pillion, the hot frost
Of an exhaust trail evaporating...

And I seem to see them both –

The dark perspex visor
Of each helmet hiding a face.

Dog Exercising Man

He sets it away widely circling across grass
Calling, again and again it comes back

Expecting reward.
When he runs zigzag to throw it off

The dog sticks to him,
Persistent in a hunt for hare...

At last it goes loping nowhere
Ignoring his coaxing to play, and he turns

Where his pregnant wife stands apart
With the child that will come between them.

At the Home

After tea left first to cool,
The mildly laxative
Cigarette, she portions out
Unchewed crusts of toast...

Shrill additions and subtractions
Have gathered at her table
Puffed soft as mufflers
In winter-thickened plumage.

Their voices are the frosty
Twitterings on chill air,
The terse asides
She takes to heart.

Sea Level

The tide is tilting in the estuary
At Tynemouth,
And the little boats bounce forward,
Skimming to the bigger sea. Against
The sea-wall the swell slops.

Here the flotsam and the jetsam
Have come to an uneasy stop:
Twigs, painted wood splinters
And the paint peeling off,
A paste of old newspapers,
Chocolate-bar wrappings:
A bloated, unknotted condom.

Today, the wind from the south
Holds them against the north sea-wall
Beneath the promontory
And the priory, the wind-peppered gravestones
Gouged, unreadable.

Nuns on a Beach

From the salty tower of a virgin king
Nuns come down to the silky beaches.

They tiptoe black-stockinged on the foreshore,
Upstaging cormorants for blackness and laughter...

And a spindly parasol twirls on its pole,
And someone points a camera,

Flummoxed at these instantaneous negatives,
Such sudden choirs of mute sea-light.

The Rock Pool

That fried egg is a jellyfish, cobalt blue,
Washed on the arc of a rock
And dead, no doubt...In this oil painting
Entitled 'Rock Pool', the rocks

Are so many joints of meat, thick-cut,
So many plucked hearts...
They look greasy, like cobblestones.
And this is a rock pool, displaced,

Part of the sea, after all –
The blanket-edge of the sea
Where the stretcher-frame ends,
And the specialist gulls reflect

On its surface, togged-out in red waders.
They have flown from the market cross,
From the podium at the centre
Of a newly constructed stadium.

They are back to add a coda
To their previous telex: a verbal report,
Intoned in geiger crackles,
Barbed, with invective.

Bad News from the North

The before-breakfast clatter of a kettle boiling,
Arthur's armoured divisions wiped clean
And that just for starters...
No longer all at one sitting,
Meals round the table together:
Their friendship soured soon enough.

*

Aneirin declining an invitation to lunch,
A self-service mead-meal at the Catterick NAAFI.
   His heroes in our mould – those
   Beautiful anatomies
   Bludgeoning one another...
And so it was he survived to tell the tale.

*

No picnic for Eric (petname: Bloodaxe)
Wanted with others for questioning.
The flight to the roof of the kingdom,
Under a cloud on Stainmore...
And there, in cars, the police were waiting,
Handing round the sandwiches.

Jacobites (1689)

Is there any, for Jesu-sake
(We heard him call from the Common)
Can help me...at Whitely Knoake,
At the fold in Gunnerton?

I want for nothing but a little help,
The relief of someone –
Someone to talk with a little,
Someone to listen.

There is one has wounded me,
And I am a dying man:
One I thought enough of to trust,
To take on an errand.

He has taken two guineas, and a crown
Piece of silver...and those spurs
I burnished this morning – gone,
Along with my gloves.

Over by the whin at the burnside
Are two grey mares tethered,
And a piece of pistol stock should be lying
Broken amidst the heather...

His two pistols: my two mares. We had
Been obliged to break cover.
Leaving the city for the highlands,
We were to cross the border.

And I had on my mind many things –
Not thinking he should shoot,
Or strike, as he did, at head and back
With each pistol butt.

I begged he lay off, and offered
All I had...I suppose
It was then, his better part
Possessed, the dark urge rose.

Grace Darling

It's as if she could countenance
Her own commemoration here,
At Bamburgh's Grace Darling Museum –
Bonneted in needlepoint, straining
At oarlocks in the portraitures.
Note: the candour of her glance
Does not out-face the visitor
But gestures, side-long – to Lonstone
Where she tended the island birds
And her watery gardens;
To that one indelible night,
Magnesium brilliant...
A trace of scalded boiler plates
Each neap tide cleanses.

Gateshead's Boer War Statue

Since those boom days, heady
With gunboat economies,
When G.M. Trevelyan invented History,
The Boer War memorial statue
Has stood at ease
Agog for an epoch: the face
The face of No-man,
The slouch hat and heavy
Moustache fashionable then
With our Imperial Yeomanry.

And it was, in school uniform,
I stood by him, scouring
The bricky veldt:
Kitchener, Roberts, Baden-Powell Street...
Those slated roofs – their raw gunmetal
Lustre, and a cordite
Stink of coal-smoke, ripening.

War Widow

Her life was one of domestic service
With a spinster in an old house on the sea-front,
Her uniform black as a funeral dress,
Her room a pre-1914 museum –
Blue patterned china, stuffed birds
In a bell-jar. It reminded her how once
She thought she saw her husband, navy blue,
Slipping through the Saturday crowds,
While on the foreshore pigeon-chested stokers
Passed the time till pubs reopened.
And how, that afternoon,
Going over things again and again,
Her snub-nosed steam iron probed,
A dreadnought through white-pleated waves.

Hewers and Putters

I

You wouldn't know, I'd hazard a guess,
That the Tyneside Scottish and the Tyneside Irish
Volunteer battalions of the '14-'18 War
Could dig trenches on the Western Front
Quicker by far than any other regiment
In the B.E.F. The reason for this,
Or so it's said, is that they were
Hewers and putters – pitmen to a man.
Those who hewed coal could dig the trenches,
While putters, in peacetime, sorted tubs. Each
In his own way skilled, they made up the rifle
Platoons and the company bombing sections.

II

On that first day of the Somme battle
Going over the top against Contalmaison
Their first objective, and leaving their second-line trench,
A scene kept well in that famous photograph,
To jaunt carelessly down the exposed
Forward slope – not many of them made it
Beyond the tangle of their own front wire.
The remainder, crossing No Man's Land,
And regrouping opposite on the German positions
A week's work of artillery had reduced
To so many shored-up narrow seams,
Dead machine gunners hunkered at their weapon –
Thirty-odd of them pushed on,
Gear in hand, hewers and putters,
As though going down to the night shift.

The Fall of France

After France what is there in forgiveness?
We have seen it all in documentary newsreel,
The whole affair mismanaged like a marriage:
The English army fallen back on Calais
Abandons scorched equipment in the sand –
They did not wash their feet or change their socks.
That private soldier who had been a baker
In peacetime kneads at soil beside his captor.

And knowing all the reasons cannot help him.

Demobilisation

It could be anywhere and miles
From where we ought to be.
The slow camber of the land,
The dominion lit at night –
A tingling constellation
Too remote to take a bearing.

Marooned
Among acres of flood water,
We drift on a world
Dissolving in rain.
My reflection at the window
Is the face of a drowned sailor.

Ward

In a grey room
Are supine figures
Gone carious with waiting.
There, angels in white
Flit along the walls,
And what appear archangels
In white flit
Along the walls
With bleepers
Bleeping...

There are those
Sleeping quietly
And other sleepers
Sighing
With something like relief.

Sailing By

They come back to us, those weather-beaten cities,
The places in the stories
Of neat spirits and unpredictable weather
Unlikely to blow over –
Of bums that freeze,
Warmed on the blubber of good company.

Come back to us...come back to us,
We are tuned-in to a signal,
A trigonometry of small-talk tingling
Like the whole nervous system
And as far as Finisterre – a frequency
Less and less decipherable each night.

...The same routines, bulletins diurnal
For those letters of marque, a three-islands
Tramp – for that old man
Wildly out on his compass bearing
And crossing the Line of Cancer to the north,
Just to catch a whiff of the vernal.

For Any Old Man

Today they are here, the young couples
Competently kissing
Where an old man in a beige raincoat
Sat on a bench to suck at his pipe,
Rewinding the spool of memory.

There is no rain but warm air today,
And fast harriers pacing
A circuit round the cemetery
Where I imagine their heel-dust sprinkling
The surface of his clay.

Grave Visiting

With no pretence
to solemnity
we erstwhile
mourners come

again to the fresh-cut grave.
No flowers
dangle from
our clammy hands.

No headstone tells
yet who it was –
only dried wreaths
like paper flowers.

We stand before
a mound of clay
collapsing
on itself...

I dreamt of him
just once –
packed in his coffin
like a orchid

in a box
he sat up and said:
I'm all right,
it's okay.

Father's Service Photograph

He is in it as it were, all present
And correct, underneath the gloss
Peak of a top-heavy naval cap:
Two spectacled monotint eyes, the family
Nose, a cheesy grin clipped back
To a faint embarrassed smile –
And the engineer's hands stuck
Gingerly behind gold braid
On the sleeves. The whole
Of his air is distracted as if
By tools above a workbench,
The years of reckonable service...

And the coffin was a lifeboat
Lowered from davits, the day
Of his sunny funeral. An image
Too late for his approval,
It fetched to mind that photograph
From the fathomless six foot under.

Walking with My Father Talking

It is as though I'm looking back, and that
Through a vision not quite 20/20. There is dust,
The brickwork of the machine shops trumped,
And a wind that picks up the dust: it talcs
The contoured slagheaps, their comforting paps...

And it is, with aid of a practical stick
I am able to dictate a diagram, still –
Say, the Doxford Reciprocating Engine,
Or point out, below, with this one
Useful arm, the wharf from which I embarked...

Yes, I have served under flags
Of once-big-names in shipping.
I have dined in their wardrooms. I have even
Stood to attention at their side
On the occasion of the surrender of empire...

Here, today, crows are circling – two black
And tatty rags against the piss-poor weather.
And I am here, full circle, an athletic invalid:
Skin a washed-out white muslin bag,
Grey lips the mush of a sodden paper cup...

And look. Here is an untended garden,
And here, an original wagon-track –
A minefield of droppings dotted about
And a difficult one to navigate...
God-suffering-shite – just look!

Day Trips

Naming the Places

Terry, tonight, in line
With Prefab Sprout,
I have, for a time, tried
Naming the places – their bricks,
Their history...in summer
A murmur of discrete hearts:
Consett...Morpeth.

Bewcastle

An age-dark recognition:
Carved legends on the cross
Worn down in a lost past,
The stranded bastle wrecked,
The sole pub locked.

Bewcastle Waste

Too much to take in at once
Of rain percolating the sikes,
Enamelling fresh meadows –
Of white bent and maiden pink
Thriving on upland moors.

Seahouses

So many false starts
Since it first began –
But the blue coble anchored
On the inner sound
Expects still to land
A crab-and-lobster catch.

Otterburn

Beneath bruised clouds, dream-
dreary islands in the sky,
two dappled warplanes clip
the nape of the wheat's blond neck:
their target today,
a distant deadman's thornbush...

At dusk – in camouflage smock,
a green cloud of foliage
and twigs – the bush is a man who up-sticks and moves off,
shouldering his bundle.

Bamburgh

A sea-fret envelops the rock
Here, where the snout of a black leather camera-case
Nuzzles the small of the sightseer's back,
Who comes to gape
Amazed at cannon muzzles,
The dream-hole in a tower-top,
Fumbling the zoom of a lens.

At his leisure, sampling the vendor's
Beefburger, he chooses this day,
This homespun animus, to take
Repossession of the city of Bebba.

Lindisfarne

From a promontory – dormant,
Warty with basalt – a belabouring
Foghorn hails its warning
To the cautious, probing boats.

Seabirds gather: cub seals,
Offshore, bark a response –
Sportive boys, and keen,
Among sunken cloisters.

62

Waren Mill

On the dank camp site
A butane burner flares
Far into the night,
Its blue flame warbling –

A cupped blossom, waiting
For neat tins in rows,
Tucked up and dozing
On a shelf in the supermarket.

On the Way

And on the way
The rose-pink asphalt B-roads,
High breeze-brushed hawthorn hedges,

And a row of low cottages
Beneath a louring sky,
Or at night the starlit beaches.

So here it is I'm caught – off guard,
At boundaries briefly glimpsed at, at edges
Crossed and recrossed.

Notes

THE PIGEON FANCIER *(page 19)*

A *cree* is a pigeon loft; *ducket* refers collectively to the roosting boxes in a pigeon loft; a bait-bag is a kind of canvas lunchbox. See Heslop's *Dictionary of Northumberland Words.*

IN THE LIT & PHIL *(page 33)*

The Literary and Philosophical Society is an eminently habitable Georgian library in the (just-off) centre of Newcastle.

BAD NEWS FROM THE NORTH *(page 47)*

There is circumstantial evidence to suggest the historical Arthur hailed from the North.

Aneirin composed the Early Welsh poem *Y Gododdin* – a people whose territory spanned N.E. England and S.E. Scotland. They were badly defeated by the Saxons at Catterick c.600 AD.

Eric Bloodaxe should need no note.

JACOBITES (1689) *(page 48)*

The substance of the poem is taken from a deposition made by the Shaftoes of Gunnerton. The unidentified man was thought to be a Jacobite agent. See Dr Edward Charlton's *Memorials of North Tynedale.*

DAY TRIPS *(page 61)*

Naming the Places: Prefab Spout is a band originally from Consett.

Bewcastle: A bastle is not quite a legitimate castle.

Bewcastle Waste: Sikes are drainage ditches, and maiden pink is a rare flower, native to Northumberland.

Seahouses: A coble is an open, clinker-built, Northumbrian fishing boat.

Bamburgh: Bebba was the Saxon Queen after whom Bamburgh is named.